T0065553

THE BANTAM
ROOSTER

PROUD AS A PEACOCK?

ADAM HOLBROOK

authorHOUSE®

AuthorHouse™
1663 Liberty Drive
Bloomington, IN 47403
www.authorhouse.com
Phone: 1 (800) 839-8640

Published by AuthorHouse 07/22/2016

ISBN: 978-1-5246-2033-2 (sc)
ISBN: 978-1-5246-2032-5 (e)

Print information available on the last page.

Any people depicted in stock imagery provided by Thinkstock are models, and such images are being used for illustrative purposes only. Certain stock imagery © Thinkstock.

This book is printed on acid-free paper.

Prologue

When I was in the military service, toward the end of the Viet Nam war, I met and was befriended by one of the few people who I ever allowed to get close enough to really know me well.

His name was Richard but he chose to be addressed as "Rich." He hailed from Atlanta, Georgia, as evidenced by his unmistakable southern manner of speech.

We considered ourselves akin to one another – blood brothers, if you will. Rich We shared many good times.

My first psychiatric hospitalization was in September of 1973 at Wright-Patterson Air Force Base near Dayton, Ohio. At that time Rich and I had been the closest friends for about six months. After a month long stint in the hospital I returned to my duty assignment in Mississippi. All I found upon my arrival there was a void in my life, a gaping abyss which the U.S. Air Force had thrown open when, in my absence, my most noble confidant was reassigned to Clark Air Base in the Philippine Islands.

I have not seen nor heard from Rich since we were separated by the call of duty so many years ago. I was almost as if he had died. I loved him as a brother and think of him often.

The one characteristic I will eternally remember about Rich is the way he would, without fail, mispronounce my name. "Holbrooks" he would call me. It wasn't "Adam" or "Holbrook" or even "Airman Holbrook." It "Holbrooks."

At the very onset of my brain sickness in the summer of 1973, while intoxicated on hard liquor and cannabis, I tried to pick a fight with Rich. That fact alone serves to prove that I was I was indeed losing my mind. Rich was six feet two and was built like Hulk Hogan. I was a mere five feet six inches tall and weighed in at one hundred twenty five pounds while soaking wet.

I, for at least twenty minutes, attempted to goad Rich into an exercise in hand to hand combat. At first he gazed in open mouthed disbelief, but the longer my tirade went on, the more amused Rich seemed to be. Suddenly, as if he could no longer restrain himself, Rich burst into a fit of laughter and shouted, "Holbrooks! You remind me of a little banty rooster!"

It is to Rich I dedicate the following work.

I

Genesis

March 31, 1954 was, as days go, most inauspicious. The sun rose, as usual. Somewhere on the face of the earth, it rained. Somewhere someone laughed Somewhere, someone wept. Somewhere a child succumbed to starvation while cradled its mother's bosom. Somewhere children played on a crumbling asphalt schoolyard. Somewhere a wounded soldier died. Somewhere a young business executive continued on his rapacious, unrelenting and remorseless way toward filching his first million dollars.

Yes, life on this planet was going on as usual. The proletariat went about as trained animals running the same mundane, utterly futile, and intrinsically fruitless rat race of living (which had been going on for centuries and to this hour) as if they had some hope of winning.

All the while the wealthy, the politicians and the socially privileged sat in the their ivory grandstand sipping dry martinis, gleefully reveling in the tragic, totally disgusting exhibition before them. They guffawed at the waste of human life and potential while an impotent clergy stood to one side with lilly white hands folded, assuring those spiritual sons of Andrew Carnegie the best places in the heavenly kingdom their money could buy.

The black-faced miners mined, the sweaty welders welded, the hungry babies cried, the cooks cooked, the waitresses served food, the truck drivers drove and the elite of society sat, with cocktails in hand, on their million dollars worth of heat rash getting richer by the minute. Yes, March 31, 1954 was in every way an ordinary day and, I suppose, as good as any to be born.

I arrived in the usual way, head first, ashen skin and (I can imagine) in excruciating pain. Some people would label me as being strong willed. That assessment of my character is quite accurate, for I displayed that trait within seconds after making my grand entrance into the world.

I refused to breathe.

The attending physician repeatedly slapped me on my wet, bloody buttocks, but wouldn't utter a sound. (I have always believed that was an absolutely brutish way of welcoming one into society. Perhaps my silence was a flaccid form of revolt. God knows.)

In desperation, the good doctor proceeded to prick my feet with pins to provoke my first cry. I took quite a few pricks of the pin, but I at last drew a deep breath and screamed in protest. All the while my dear, delirious mother was lying flat on her back demanding that those people stop sticking pins in her baby.

I have no way of proving it, but I suspect the old codger stuck me once more for good measure even after my caterwauling filled every corner of the delivery room. Perhaps it was his way of getting even with this impudent little butt head who had dared to defy him.

As was Levon (let the Elton John fans understand.) I was born "a pauper to a pawn" and even today that fact is a source of distempered pride that I have flaunted in the face of many wealthy people. Not that anyone really takes joy in being poor, but it requires infinitely a greater degree of moral fiber to be reared in poverty than it does to be born into the lap of luxury.

As you may by now suspect, my roots are deeply embedded in the much less than fertile soil of the working class. My father was a steel foundry maintenance man and my mother an erstwhile waitress at the time of my birth. My folks were both of eastern Kentucky heritage and having my mother rear me in that atmosphere has had, and still has today, a profound impact upon my life and greatly influenced my long held core beliefs.

Speaking of being reared, I was taught in elementary school that children are not raised – they are reared. Believe me, in my growing up years I was reared quite a few times.

Yes, thee have been moments of despair in which I curse the day I was conceived in the womb of my mother. But I do

3

now feel deeply indebted to my parents for granting me the gift of life. Most of the ills of society, corporately and individually, stem from the misunderstanding and misuse of that gift.

Yes, life is a gift. It is not ours for the taking, excepting in extreme cases as delineated very clearly in our state and federal statues.

Life is not to be squandered, spent in the pursuit of idle pleasures or to be employed for the singular purpose of making others miserable. It is not to be dedicated as a tool for the appeasement of one's devilish lust for power. Not is it to be misapplied in a headlong mad dash toward senseless extravagance purchased by the blood, sweat and tears of the less fortunate. Those who do these things are missing the point entirely.

Then, of course, at the opposite end of the social spectrum are those who stand bovine faced, day after day in long lines at government handout stations waiting to be spoon fed their daily dose of pabulum. I was in that position for enough time to realize that life is not for that either. That is why I endeavor to write books and give speeches. I was almost twenty years old when stricken with mental illness and when life throws you lemons you can do one (or both) of two things. You can throw them back or make lemonade. Right?

What is the cure for the creeping paralysis which is devouring America? Simply this: Change a man's heart and you have changed his destiny. Change man's individual destiny and you have changed the destiny of of the nation – one heart at a time.

II

Death's Door

Most of us would rather not entertain in our frail minds the fact that death is an inevitable part of living. As much as we all, as physically finite beings, would rather push the reality of death as far out of our consciousness as possible, the certainty of death remains. Although we are the highest form of life that God has placed on this earth, we share a common bond with all other living things – as surely as our physical bodies are living, they will one day die.

We homo sapiens are the most egocentric and self absorbed form of life on this planet. We see ourselves as invincible, as being above all natural laws, including the law of physical death. It is as if, in the human psyche, death is in some peculiar way equated with defeat. The exact opposite is true. For those who have developed a personal relationship with God, bodily death is the ultimate victory. It is simply a promotion to glory.

Nevertheless, we all remain accountable to life. The fact we are here places a demand on us which, if disregarded or shirked, we fail to live up to out full human potential as daughters and sons of God.

I had just arrived on planet earth when my life was nearly taken from me by something as simple as an infantile case of pertussis. I contracted the ailment from a group of snotty nosed neighbor children who insisted on meeting the new baby.

The way my mother described the scene, that grubby troop of children paraded into the bedroom and surrounded my bassinet, all the while coughing, sneezing and wheezing all over themselves and anyone else who happened to be in a ten foot radius. Mother had refused, up to that time to allow those germ laden little mongrels to come near me. But on that particular day she was coerced by their mother who had become indignant because her little darlings had been heretofore been denied access to my sleeping quarters.

My becoming ill came as no surprise to my mother. My two older siblings had contracted pertussis (as had seemingly every child within a six square block radius of our apartment house) and as nature took its course I came down with the ailment also.

As any good mother would have done, Mom took her three children to see a physician who prescribed the appropriate medications. The doctor sent us home with assurances to Mom that we would be fine.

All seemed well until shortly before ten the next morning mother looked in on me and discovered that I was not breathing. My lips and nail beds were blue. Mother scooped me up and dashed down the narrow stairway, shouting as she went.

Across the street was our fifteen year old neighbor was washing his care and probably thinking of the day when he could legally drive it. When he heard Mother screaming with a blue baby in her arms, he ran into the house to get his mother. The neighbor lady ran across the street and into our building shouting at Mom she would care for the other children.

With Mother, who was clutching my lifeless body, the young man sped away to St. Rita Medical Center.

"You don't have a license!" Mother shouted to the young driver.

"Then we'll have a police escort!" he shouted back.

The hospital staff had no way of knowing that we were coming, but as Mother stepped through the emergency room door a nurse snatched me from her arms and hurriedly dashed down the hallway. The place came alive as doctors, nurses and other medical personnel came running from seemingly out of nowhere. On her way down the corridor, a frantic nurse called to a pair of Catholic sisters who were standing nearby.

"Get the priest, go to the chapel and *pray!*"

A doctor who was on duty at that time performed a tracheotomy, cutting a hole in my throat through which I could breathe. (To this day I have a deep scar on my throat just below my Adam's apple. Since that time, I have two other operations on my throat. One was another tracheotomy, the other was to have a portion of my trachea removed.)

So intense were the doctor's efforts, e ripped sutures from his right hand which had been laid open a few days earlier by a lawn mower blade. As he introduced the plastic tube though the opening in my throat, my mother heard the doctor whisper, "Come on little guy, *Breathe!*"

It. Worked. Everyone's prayers were answered. Baby boy Holbrook revived.

What had happened was the mucus had blocked my windpipe just above my larynx. Once the tracheotomy had been performed and the tube inserted I began to draw shallow breaths. However, since my brain had been without oxygen for an undetermined period of time, there was great concern of my having severe and permanent brain damage.

My father had been summoned from work and as he and Mother waited to hear from the doctor, they hoped..... and prayed. After what seemed to be eternity, the doctor emerged from the elevator with a grim expression on his face.

"Your baby is alive and in a oxygen tent." the doctor reported. "But" he continued, "if he lives beyond this afternoon he will be severely retarded."

Although some of them are under te impression they are God, doctors can be wrong. In spite of such a bleak diagnosis, Mother never let her faith waiver. I believe it was her faith which preserved me then and continues to preserve me though the many challenges I face in life.

My recovery was dramatic and with so few signs of brain damage, the hospital staff referred to me as "the miracle baby." That should not come as a surprise. I was born a fighter. Even as an infant, through the power of God I had defied the odds and won.

Now, I will admit to you there are times when I slide into despair and become very bitter toward the apparently divine invention which kept me alive. Sometimes it seems to me that things had been much better if I had spent the last sixty or so years in heaven rather than on this perfectly horrid hunk of rock called earth.

At times I squirm and whine under the hand of God's eternal purpose. Although growing up amid the splendors of heaven would have been far more pleasant than growing up in this cock-eyed, tipsy-turvey, out of kilter world, I still just can't help but believe there is an eternal purpose for my sojourn here.

It's not that I am some sort of heavenly gift to mankind, you understand, but *every* child who is born into this hostile, cold blooded, hard boiled and compassion-less world has come here by divine appointment. Every person on this planet has the potential to make better his or her world.

God's eternal purpose for each individual person can be (and more often than not) thwarted by any one of the following: insensitive (and/or willfully ignorant) parents, cruel school mates, bad role models, incompetent (and/or immoral clergy), hateful school teachers the horrors of asinine wars, and myriads of other adverse conditions. But each person nonetheless remains a person of destiny.

Whether or not that destiny is fulfilled depends not so much upon outward circumstances, although they do have a definite influence, but it depends mostly on not the outside – but the inside of a person. Call it The Force if you like, a life source, the spirit of God or whatever you choose to call it, is inborn and common to all people.

Some people simply surrender under the weight of so many years of adversity (the extreme of this is suicide) while others will fight to the point they feel they are drawing their last breath. They survive and ultimately go on to enjoy a good life. Why?

Why do some people overcome seemingly impossible odds and go on to live productive lives, while others spend their lives in misery or resort to suicide? Why do some choose to struggle for years and overcome devastating circumstances (Joni Earickson Tada comes to mind) while some collapse under the slightest hint of hardship?

I have been confined with psychiatric patients my own age who have been institutionalized for years were very contented. All I could think of was getting out of there and doing something with my life, even if that was pumping gasoline for a living. I was, at that time, every bit as unbalanced as they were. They remain to this day unbalanced and hospitalized. I do not. What made the difference?

I have no fast and easy answers. I have no magic formula for success. Nor do I have a crystal ball to gave into for guidance. This not really a self-help book because I am certainly not found my way our of the woods yet, psychologically speaking. I can truthfully also say that my life was not and is not a smashing success (yet). Neither is my life that ever-elusive bed of roses that many speak of but few experience. I will say, however, what most people experience in life is due to the choices they have made. God knows I have made my share of regretful choices, which have led me down some very rough roads, some where even angels fear to tread.

But when confronted with an obstacle, I just smile and affirm to myself, "This makes me *strong!*" If you practice this consistently, before long, even before you know it, you will be strong enough to scale any mountain life puts in your way. Try it!

Another trite, but true, saying that I have applied to my life is this, "Big shots are little shots who keep shooting." No matter what you do, do it the best of your ability and don't stop.

I know of a man in Findlay, Ohio who started out riding a garbage truck but became successful in the refuse removal business within just a few years. He simply refused to stop shooting. But this man, as I do, measures success not id dollars and cents, but as to what degree he is respected, trusted and loved.

Don't delude yourself into believing you must have a mega-bucks job or profession to consider yourself successful. That's the way the world thinks and remember this world is a messed up place. Most of the things the world sees as valuable are, in fact, worthless. It all depends on the way you choose to look at things.

What is a diamond? A diamond is nothing more than a good looking rock. My two little daughters find pretty rocks behind our garage every day. Diamonds are here for us to admire – not worship. As Dion DiMucci said in one of his songs, "Cadillac s end up in the junk yard."

September 7, 1997

I started this chapter called *Death's Door* months ago and in that time of absence from my desk have developed an entirely new perspective of what it means to be literally at death's door and it was quite an eye-opener.

You see, I had open heart surgery on May 30, 1997. I was in a coma and as good as dead from then until July 8, 1997. Post-operative complications, which included a usually fatal condition called Acute Respiratory Distress Syndrome (ARDS) nearly took me down.

It is only by God's grace that I am living and able to write these words. God proved his love for my friends and loved one as well. He spared them the sorrow my death would have brought.

Just as my perspective on death has changed, so my perspective on life has changed. My life means more to me now than it ever did. I have a new love for my wife and children, the likes of which was formerly unknown to me.

Have my circumstances changed? Not really I still live in the same house on the same street in the same town. I still own the same Dodge minivan that I owned several months ago. My wife is the same person she was. She hasn't changed her hairstyle or her taste in clothing. Have my children suddenly become living proof that angelic beings dwell among men? Hardly!

My circumstances have not at all changed, but I *have*. I have come to the conclusion that people were not just blowing smoke when the said, "Life is what you make it." or "You get out of life what you put into it."

I am not at all suggesting that depressed people need to experience (God forbid) a five week coma in order to see things differently. Good mental health professionals and/or the right medication can go a long way toward acquiring a healthy view of life. But spending hours with a therapist and popping pills by the dozen will not do much good until the person consciously *decides* to take a new lease on life. It took a near death experience to cause me to come to this conclusion. I pray it doesn't take that kind of experience to bring you around.

Seemingly eons ago, when I grudgingly began work on this book I possessed an outlook on life similar to that of a proctologist. Recalling my health crisis of last summer I now have the outlook of a pediatrician. That is, I see new life every day. Like a child in the care of a trusted physician life can be beautiful and it rarely has any sort of malady that can not be remedied.

III

Early Times

In writing this chapter, I do feel much like a time traveler. Voyaging back though time and space in the theater of my mind finds me at various times, in many diverse places with many different people. Many recollections of people, places and events evoke a feeling of warm contentment an inward joy. Others make me want to laugh and still others bring me to the brink of tears.

All of us possess the power to regress to bygone years and relive happenings in the past much as they happened. The ability to wander backward in time by means of memory should perhaps be one of the most cherished gifts which the Almighty has bestowed upon us. Sadly, the power to remember can be a curse. Some individuals rarely exercise this power because doing so is far too painful an experience.

To these unfortunate ones being an intracranial time traveler only dredges up shadowy figures from days gone by they would just as soon forget. These specters from their personal antiquity haunt them every minute of every day and the prickly weeds of former times chafe their already bruised and bleeding souls.

I, like many people have had perhaps more than my share of these prickly weeds to contend with. However, through the grace of God, I have endeavored to see these painful events through the panoramic lens of a renewed mind. These memories are much less tormenting when viewed from the divine perspective. That is, getting the big picture in the light of eternity.

Yes, I have had some nightmarish things happen over the years. But now I view those experiences as sign posts I have passed on the road to becoming the person I am today and point the way to the better person I will be tomorrow.

Having been chided as "Arnold Acne" by my peers on the school bus has caused me to have compassion on those who are not as attractive as society would have them be. Having experienced years of anguish due to the horrors of mental illness has caused me to hurt along with those who, through no fault of their own, have had the very soul ripped out of themselves and are coping with that pain by withdrawal into psychosis. Have been homeless allows me to relive the fearful things street people endure every day and thus minister to their spiritual needs.

I, like far too many others, have been ostracized, jilted, made sport of, divorced, homeless, driven out of my mind (literally), rendered helpless by prescription drugs, burned out by street drugs, heart broken, put down, put out, trodden under the feet of society and hated for no good reason.

I have, as countless other socially tyrannized individuals, lived through being psychologically wrung out, my soul and spirit stretched beyond the outer limits of human endurance.

But, do you know what I have found? It is only the ones who sail through life happy, prosperous, outwardly attractive (but inwardly hideous) carefree, successful and with a million things going for them at birth who merit my pity.

Why? Because the only thing which breeds pure compassion is excruciating personal experience. They have never once suffered a broken heart. They have never, late at night, fallen on their faces in the darkness and cried out in physical and/or emotional anguish. They have never truly hurt. These people have never had to struggle to the top of the mountain. They were born there. They will never experience the exhilarating view from the top of the mountain after having made the climb. It is for those people I sincerely feel sorry because they have never and will never and in fact can never know the depths of human compassion. Don't let the hard knocks of life make you bitter. Let them make you better.

Although it is sometimes distressing, time traveling can be fun. I am delighted you have decided to come along.

Meandering back to my earliest recollections, it is firm belief the very first words to become a permanent part of my ever-expanding vocabulary were, "Go *home* Frankie!" These three words were oft repeated by my mother throughout my first three or so years and were reserved for use whenever an obnoxious little neighbor boy by the name of Frankie appeared on our doorstep, which seemed to be every ten minutes.

Frankie was a toe-headed little monster who belonged to a slatternly delegation who made their home in the apartment building located directed in front of our cottage. Both structures were located on the corner of St. Johns Avenue and Fourth Street in Lima, Ohio roughly in the year of our Lord 1955.

The small cottage in which we lived is still standing, although now it is being used as storage space for Army's Auto Wrecking. The larger building which housed Frankie and company has long since been razed, rendering homeless perhaps thousands of cockroaches.

Sometime in the year 1955, mu mother an father were, for a reason that has never been made clear to me, divorced. Mother was granted custody of my sister, Rhonda, and yours truly. It was also decided that my brother, Paul Micheal would remain with our father. Rhonda, the first born in our family is four years older than me. Paul Micheal (or Mike) is two years my senior.

In my early years I developed a rather peculiar habit. Much to the disconcert ion of my oft embarrassed mother, I staunchly persisted in clutching the crotch of my bib-overalls as if I had the urge to urinate. In fact Mother had an old photograph of the St. Johns Avenue gang and there I am on the front row, scowling as if weaned on pickle juice and - you guessed it- gripping my private parts.

Mother could, without fail, discern whether I was merely holding myself (for whatever reason) or truly needed to use the restroom. If I genuinely had to go, I would abruptly break into a variation of the hula, tug on Mother's dress hem and yell for all the world to hear, "Mommy!! I'm 'bout to *pee!!*"

The knitting of my eyebrows together while glowering at the world seemed to be a permanent part of my demeanor in those days. Nothing said or done could cause me to smile. At the age of two years I had developed a very sour outlook on life as evidenced by the aforementioned photograph. I was quite an unpleasant little fellow and nothing seemed to please me.

When perusing over my old pictures, I often wonder if it is at all possible for a three or four year old child to suffer from depression. I have been prone to be depressed as far back as I can remember and have been on medication for that malady (and schizophrenia) for quite a few years.

In the course of my most recent hospitalization (and I have had many), I found myself conversing with a lady who told me her father died of depression. I looked at her quizzically and asked, "Depression?" I could see much pain come onto her face as she choked on these words, "Yes.... depression....my Dad Committed suicide.....when I was sixteen."

At that moment the reality of depression being a fatal disease struck me very hard. It was quite an emotional slap to realize the black cloud under which I had lived so many years could have killed me. I have had two attempts and executed suicidal gestures, but I had never come to grips with why until that day.

Thinking back over my life, I discovered that as a young woman my mother displayed symptoms of being profoundly depressed and no means to gain relief. In this enlightened age of designer medications, new talk therapy techniques, and progressive psychiatric hospitals there is at least a ray of hope in the middle of our agony. But as for Mom in the nineteen fifties and sixties there was little, if any hope available. There were no community mental health centers, no wonder drugs or latest medical breakthroughs to guide the doctors. There was also (and still is to a great extent) the social stigma of being under the care of a psychiatrist. The best any disturbed person could look forward to was months, or perhaps years, confined to a hellish government operated institution.

Incidentally, I have done time in a few government operated psychiatric facilities. They are much improved from what they were when I became ill forty two years ago. As I have said though, back then the treatment for mental illness was in the stone age. I am thankful the outlook for the mentally ill is getting brighter every day. I also give thanks to my mother who went through a private hell alone, coping as best she could, reared her children and came out on the other side.

IV

God's Country

The scene now shifts from a small squalid cottage on St Johns Avenue to a forty acre plot of ground located nine miles southeast of Lima on State Route 117, a quarter of a miles south of the village of Westminster, Ohio. Mom always affectionately referred to as "Gods" Country. The farm was about three hundred feet off the road and could only be accessed by means of a narrow, unpaved, sparsely graveled lane.

Mom and Bob had exchanged wedding vows in September of 1965 and the following spring we moved out of the city to the farm. Our 'farm" consisted of several dilapidated sheds, a hog house in the woods (plus a tin corn crib), a red shingled out house and the one room shanty where we lived. Mom sometimes characterized our house as a "reconverted chicken coop."

My now deceased grandfather-in-law, when passing by our farm (as our new house was being constructed) remarked, "What do you know? They're buildin' a house back there. Those people were livin' in a chicken coop!" My wife was a nine year old child at that time and remembers thinking to herself, "*Nobody* lives in a chicken coop!":

It was great fun living in the wide open spaces. I learned my numbers early on by helping Bob count his pigs as they arrived at the hog house for dinner. At the age of five I witnessed the miracle of birth by assisting Bob in delivering a litter of piglets.

Along with each litter of those darling little flat nosed grunters there came one runt which we would bring inside the house so as to protect the little booger from its stronger siblings. The one runt I most vividly remember is was the rascal Rhonda named "Pinky." We gave all of the runts lots of TLC (tender loving care) but sadly, being born sick, they were only able survive for more than a week or so.

One thing that always has amazed me about swine is how the little ones can be born so endearing but grow to be more utterly repulsive the closer they come to adulthood. Looking at things realistically, through casual observation, I find that some humans display the same characteristic.

One of the things I recall most vividly were the farm auctions that Bob and I religiously attended. It seemed we found one very few weeks.

I will describe the scene as through the eyes of a five year old. There was a man standing on a farm wagon who was shouting at a deafening decibel level through a makeshift public address system. His speech was so rapid that he was, no doubt, a court reporter's nightmare. That man, Bob explained, was the auctioneer. (I have encountered telemarketers who missed their calling. They'd have made outstanding auctioneers.) Standing on each side of the auctioneer there were two other men who would, every few seconds, point to someone in the crowd and shout "*HIP*!!"

All of this made very little sense to me then, but I loved the auctions because Bob would without fail buy me at least one bottle of orange soda, or in cold weather multiple cups of hot cocoa. Going to the auction also meant hauling home at lest one corroded washtub full of junk in which I always found a toy or two.

As a child I looked forward to Easter with as much anticipation as I did Christmas. In years gone by, Easter was celebrated weeks later than it is now. Easters of yesteryear were usually observed observed under favorable weather conditions which made for a day of frolicking in the sun.

East meant a get-together with my cousins. Theses gatherings came complete with an abundance of candy, an Easter egg hunt and usually a good scolding for getting my new clothes dirty. Easter marked a milestone also because it was the one Sunday of the year when Mom could successfully persuade Bob to attend church.

One Easter in my early years, Rhonda and I were presented with two yellow, down covered, adorable ducklings. Living in the country meant we had the proper resources to keep them. In those days many department stores embraced the thoroughly disgusting practice practice of giving away ducklings or chicks at Easter. Due to an expanded public awareness of animal rights the giving away of young animals has been abandoned.

I crowned my duckling Hector and probably because his relatively short time among the living, I don't recall what name Rhonda gave her duck.

On one balmy spring day, shortly after the ducks arrived, Mother gave me the order to go out and water the ducks. Being the obedient child I was taught to be, I proceeded to carry out her instructions. Hector slurped up the water as if he had three weeks in Death Valley, but Rhonda's duck didn't seem to be the least bit interested in having a drink of cool well water.

This perturbed me. I mean, I had gone to all the trouble to pump the water from the well (a strenuous procedure for one so young), then lug that heavy bucket of water fifty feet to the duck pen and that ingrate refused to drink. I felt most insulted, so I decided to force the issue.

"*Drink* duck!" I shouted as I held his downy head under the water for nearly three minutes. Bubbles began to flow from the small holes in the duckling's bill. Satisfied the duck had had his fill, I released his head. To my astonishment, he flopped over, motionless, on his side.

I suddenly came to the realization that I had drowned Rhonda's duck. As tears stung my freckled face I ran to the house. Rhonda forgave me and I promised to share the surviving duck.

Being a small child on an isolated farm had its downside though. After two years on the farm Rhonda left us to live with Dad in Kenton, Ohio and I was left alone.

Being alone much of the time was maddening, especially when Bob was away working. Bob was the only "Buddy" I had. In his absence I had to find some means of entertaining myself. As a result, I withdrew into the whimsical world of my imagination.

God only knows the number of fire breathing dragons that were slain, the auto races were won, the damsels in distress who were rescued and the aerial dog fights which broke out on our little parcel of God's country.

Sadly though one of the greatest endowments God had given me at an early age lies dead and buried as of autumn of 1973. Although in partial remission, schizophrenia has robbed me of many things, among those being my capacity to visualize and create.

The ability to envisage, to take nothing more than a fleeting thought and develop it into a work of art, a new concept, a a new product or service is a God given gift that should by no means ever be misused or misdirected.

People nowadays are employing the precious resource of their minds to create the vulgar, the ugly, the violent and the obscene. Remember that in the days before the great flood all human life (save eight persons) was destroyed because the very imagination of the human race was engaged for evil purposes. If the mental faculties of a person are bent on evil, his actions and words will reflect that evil. As Evangelist Andrew Wommack has said, "You cannot be tempted with anything you can't imagine."

V

Little Adam

It is just after 11 pm. On March 1, 1996. My daughter's fifth birthday party is over. The little guests have long since gone home and I am left alone with my thoughts and my word processor.

I received a telephone call today from a magazine publisher in a small town near Philadelphia. She was interested in ding a piece on my first two books, *Dear Mom* and *Shining On* in her magazine. In the course of our conversation Kate, the publisher, told me of her seven-year-old son whom she and her husband had adopted. He was at that time in a psychiatric hospital undergoing treatment. The little fellow's birth mother had named him Adam.

As many mentally ill persons are, little Adam was described by his adopted mother to be extremely intelligent and immensely talented in the area of art. Kate related to me that although what Adam depicted in his artwork was often appalling, his works definitely revealed that he was gifted far beyond his years.

When Kate and her husband adopted little Adam, they were told that he had been abused by his birth mother and her live-in boyfriend and, as a result, suffered some emotional difficulty. Kate and her husband are both clinical psychologists, so they agreed to take Adam feeling confident they could help him to adjust and resolve his inner turmoil. They were not prepared for what they soon encountered after the adoption.

They had been told that Adam had been abused, but they were not fully informed how much and what kind of abuse he had suffered. They discovered this little fellow had been abused in every way imaginable – sexually abused, physically tortured, both psychologically and physically raped. This all was done in ways that are indescribably gruesome and reading about it is apt to nauseate the strongest of people, so I swill spare you.

Incidentally, Adam had a six month old half sister who was bludgeoned to death before the authorities could remove the children from the household.

At the time I spoke with Kate little Adam had been institutionalized because his behavior had become violently suicidal and homicidal.

What breaks my heart is there may thousands of children like Adam out there. So I do what most people do – I try not to think about them. The government says of every problem, "Throw a little money at it and it will go away." We have to date spent massive amounts of money in a feeble effort to eliminate child abuse, but the problem has not gone away. If anything it has gotten worse. The solution to the child abuse problem is not only money, but caring and skilled professionals who know how to treat not only small children, but the whole family.

November 24, 1996

In my days of severe depression, I would sit and whine to myself (my wife refused to listen to my self-indulgent polyglot) about how I was abused. I have had several therapists ask me point blank, "Were you abused?" The answer is yes, and no. Were your parents good parents – yes and no.

Why the ambivalence? Because, as I have previously stated, my mother suffered from what appeared to be deep depression at a time when treatment options were few. I found that when I was depressed my parenting skills went out of the window. I related to my children much in the same way my mother related to men I was torn between being a loving parent and a frustrated, hateful person who wanted not to be hassled with looking after children.

Do I love my children? Of course I do. I'd give my life for them. Did Mom love me? Of course she did. I can now grasp the full scope of what my dear mother went through. The difference being I had help in coping with my depression. Mom didn't.

Later on, in my adolescence, the most abuse was at the hands of my school classmates who refuse to address me as in any way other than *Arnold Acne* or *Hey Arnold!*

When Mother and stepfather realized how badly I was being mistreated because of an severe case of acne they took me, at great expense, to a dermatologist. Within three months I was nearly cured. Yes, there are emotional wounds stemming from my adolescence. I can't really say for certain even now if the cuts and bruises are healed.

Also, at home, my folks had a difficult time dealing with a sometimes mouthy, goofy, klutzy, moody, insufferable, rebellious, shiftless, and pimply teenager.

Mom and Bob chose to deal with me by means of heavy handed discipline. In some teens this method can be quite effective. In other cases it can be an unmitigated disaster. My folks dealt with me *the best way they knew how.* They had the right motives and that, my friend, is what is important.

I can sum up my childhood and adolescence by quoting two lines from Charles Dickens' magnificent work, A tale of Two Cities:

They were the best of times......

They were the worst of times.....

VI

Celebrations

Little more than a week ago my family and I attended a celebration. It was one which overflowed with joy, love, tearful greetings, and hugs. A company of friends and neighbors from Westmi9nster, Ohio and it's environs had gathered to pay tribute to a truly remarkable man on his seventy-fifth birthday., that man being my stepfather. Robert J. "Bob" Aab.

At that get-together I beheld the aging but radiant faces of my lifelong friends and their parents. These were all people who had known me practically from the time I was being potty trained. These people, all of them, had in some way influenced the life of this aspiring writer and when remembering these people these persons, I can't help give in to the nostalgic frame of mind and long for "Home," that being Westminster as it was years ago.

The aged men sat, day after day and hour after hour on the white wooden bench in front of Zimmerman's General Store whittling away sticks of wood as well as the hours of the day. Children were everywhere. The trees which lined the streets were lush and green.

The Westminster of my early years was teeming with life and vitality. It was home to a close-knit community of simple, hasrd working folks who had formed from that village a family of sorts. Everyone looked to the welfare of the other. These was no need for food stamps. Mr. Zimmerman saw to it that those who were having hard times had groceries. Mr. Fisher (who owned the service station in the town made certain that all has gasoline enough until payday. Ast The Canary Restaurant there was always of bowl of hot soup or cup of coffee for the elderly gentlemen who stopped by.

I could go on *ad infinitum* about the Westminster of yesteryear, but the village of that time was in my childhood and my childhood is long since over. Now the streets of that once quaint little hamlet are practically deserted. The old folks who I know have gone, each his to his or her eternal reward and the once middle-aged people are now the elderly. Mr. Zimmerman has closed the store and moved on to his much deserved retirement. Mr. Fisher's service station is now used as storage space for the Rudolph Foods company, which the old timers still refer to as "the peanut factory."

The local children have grown up and mostly gone to seek their fortune in greener pastures. The trees which once flourished along the streets have all been trimmed back to the bare nubbins and will take some time to recover.

I left that birthday party nearly in tears. I felt as though I would weep for joy of once last time seeing al those people who had, in effect brought all the way from boyhood to being a proud young soldier and beyond. I also felt as though I would weep for sorrow because that village of barely three hundred people which held so many cherished memories is so much different now. It seemed as though westminster had grown old with its inhabitants.

Not long before that, Mary and I departed another gathering in tears. This one was held in an out of the way second floor gallery called "The Loft" in Ft. Wayne, Indiana. It was a conclave of artists, relatives, friends and other interested persons who had came pay tribute to a multi-talented young man who, at the age of twenty one, died as the result of his mental illness.

I had never met Justin Blessing, but became acquainted with his father, Tom Blessing, in October 1996. Tom and were part of a part of a radio panel discussion of mental illness. It was then I heard, as the radio listeners did, Justin's heart rending story.

Mr. Blessing spoke of his son's talents and all he had accomplished in his abbreviated life. He had played the lead role in a drama, *The Crucible*, in his senior year at Homestead High School inj Ft. Wayne. A few years earlier he had played the narrator in the, *"Our Town"*. Mr. Blessing also told of Justin's gift in the field of art. Justin was attending one of the most prestigious art school in the country when he was incapacitated by mental illness. The diagnosis: Schizophrenia

Tom Blessing told of Justin's eighteen month struggle with his illness. The described the three steps forward, two steps back process of his son's illness. This is a very common occurrence with mental illness.

But, due to drowsiness and other effects of the prescribed medication (which could possibly have been his salvation) Justin voluntarily discontinued their use. They stifled his creativity, he said. They made him spend to much time sleeping, he said, not realizing these and other side effects were temporary and would diminish in the course of his treatment.

Ultimately, Justin was seen walking unsteadily along a busy thoroughfare near Ft. Wayne, disheveled and confused. He had left home to visit his sister but had gotten lost. He drove until his automobile ran out of fuel, then he took to walking. Justin was two policemen in two separate instances, but was not taken into custody (as he should have been) and transported to a hospital where he could have found treatment. And been safe.

Justin Blessing, the talented, the gifted, the talented and the friend of many had been reduced to being a babbler wandering the streets in the rain with no food, drink or shelter for thirty six hours. He was, in reality, homeless.

I often wonder if those who passed by and turned up their noses at this pathetic "bum" had any idea of the exceptional mind this young man, until recently, had possessed. Was he just another freeloader? Was he just another canker sore on the upper lip of society? Hardly!

But that is what people thought they were passing as they saw him meandering, perhaps staggering, down the road last evening. *"Ugh!* Another *bum*! They are coming out of the woodwork for Gawd's sake."

I also thought of there being cruel persons who laid on their car horn button just to scare this *bum*.

One can only imagine the number of people, some perhaps with gifts comparable to Justin, who have walked the streets of our cities for years eating out of trash dumpsters and sleeping through sub-zero temperatures in cardboard hovels. They suffer from an incurable – but entirely treatable disease.

Any treatise on mental illness would be incomplete without at least a cursory remarking on the vast quagmire of the health insurance industry's policies concerning brain disorders. Check your health insurance coverage of what it will pay toward the treatment of diabetes. Then do the same with brain disorders. See the differences even though mental illness is, as is diabetes, due to a chemical imbalance in the body.

This idiotic double standard was common among insurance providers until just a few years ago. This is something which is reluctantly being changed. Tom Blessing and I could together write volumes on the subject of medical coverage for brain sickness. Enough said, at least now.

When Mary and I arrived at *The Loft* that evening, I immediately perceived that Tom Blessing's admiring comments about his son were not empty results of the "proud papa" syndrome. Lining the walls were sixty or so paintings and drawings done by Justin. What struck me first was the variety of the art media employed and the diverse subject matter. There were works which many would call abstract alongside of art that blared of stark realism. The several self portraits were finely detailed and stunning.

After Justin's family had thanked all in attendance and had read poems composed by Justin, his brother-in-law (John Rogers) and another equally adept guitarist gave a short acoustic guitar concert.

Then a video presentation, which was edited by Justin's sister Adrianne, was projected on a large flat screen television screen. Featured were clips of Justin's drama performances from his elementary school years through high school. The video segments we viewed were outstanding by anyone's standard.

About seven minutes into the film I suddenly was reminded of the fact that this Hollywood quality young actor had left this earth many years too soon. I was, as well as Mary deeply moved, our hearts touched in a somehow inexplicable way.

Neither Mary and I had much to say to one another as we left *The Loft* that evening. What we had seen of young Justin's work rendered both of us in a very contemplative mood, as though we needed time to fully process what we had seen and heard.

Justin Blessing's short life had come to an end in the driving rain on a desolate stretch of highway. This side of heaven we will never know precisely what Justin's demented mind was telling him when he laid himself down on the rain slickened roadway. Perhaps he lost consciousness due to exhaustion and dehydration. No one knows for certain how long he lay there before he was run over and killed by a hit and run diver.

Dear God, move us to seek out and give light to the Justins of this world. The world of the mentally ill is a very dark and rainy place. I know. I left Ft. Wayne that night a changed in the sense that I am decidedly more determined to be an encouragement, a support, a friend, an advocate, a political activist, or anything I must be in order to bring hope and life to the mentally ill and their families. Having experienced the depths of mental illness myself, it is the least I can do for the Justins of this world and those like him.

VII

Rainy Days

March 10, 1997 2:39 am

I don't really feel much like writing, but I need to at least offer some feeble excuse for an attempt to finish this book. You have by now read about my step-father Bob in the preceding chapters (and perhaps in my other books). Well, Bob had open heart surgery a week ago. This came hot on the heels of my Aunt Audrey (Mother's sister)undergoing the same procedure and passed away a few days post-op. Don't fret yourself about Bob though. He is a tough old bird who came through like a champ.

I have never in my writings mentioned a good deal about natural father, Reverend Gale Holbrook. That is probably because I didn't know him well enough to have much to say. He was an ordained minister of the old-fashioned Pentecostal persuasion for many years. Dad was an old stalwart who stood y what he believed, come what may.

I was nineteen years old before I spent a night in his home. Still, on my birthday and at Christmas Dad always came with presents in hand and was ever-faithful in being prompt with his child support payments even though I know making those payments was a real hardship for him and his new family.

As I have mentioned, Dad and Mom were divorced when I was very young. Dad remarried afterward, as did Mom. Mother married Robert (Bob) Aab and Dad married a young by the names of Barbara Fields. Due to an illness, Bob and Mom never had children together, but Dad fathered two more girls and a set of twin boys who died shortly after birth.

As I said in a previous chapter, Mom suffered greatly from what was probably acute depression. Bob was quite capable of being a loving and kind man. He was a decorated World War II veteran who was equally prone to be as gruff, crude and seemingly cruel as he was gentle.

When I was in elementary school we were given the assignment of committing to memory the preamble to the U.S. Constitution. When I read over it in class I was perplexed as to the meaning of the phrase. "to insure domestic tranquility" I raised my hand as asked what it meant. Our teacher, whose husband was a Methodist minister, replied by saying it meant "tp insure peace in the home' (which I thought was a real cop-out). I came back at her saying "George Washington and those guys didn't know what they were talkin' about! There's *always* somebody raisin' hell at our house!"

It doesn't require a good deal of imagination to know what happened next.

Our household was a real paradox. It could be a real hell hole at times, but there was a great deal of bonding in the family. We were held by a mutual bond of real affection even though Mother, with little or no provocation could explode into a screaming fit. Bob, a muscular man, could swing a belt with the best of them. Through all of that disorder, odd it may seem, we were held together as a family with indissoluble chords of love.

But getting back to Dad, the only way describe him is to borrow a phrase from the U.S. Marine Corp, *Semper Fideles* – always faithful. Dad was indeed faithful to his God, the people that he pastored, his spouse, his children and never once compromised his convictions, no matter what the cost.

The last time I saw Dad was about seven hours ago as he lay dying in a Cleveland area hospital. As I am writing this the time is 3:56 am and Dad may have already passed on to glory. That doesn't bother me much because I know the first thing he will hear as he arrives will be, "Well done! My good and faithful servant!"

March 20, 1997 1:26 am

On the afternoon of March 10, 1977 the Reverend Gale Holbrook died. His funeral was held on March 14 in the same church where he had accepted Christ years before.

I could probably write an entire chapter on the rich heritage on that quaint country chapel called Quickstep Pentecostal Church. (It was named Quickstep because the road on which it is located was once known as Quickstep

Road. As a child I believed that church was named Quickstep in reference to the fancy dancing some Pentecostal people do when they are "in the spirit.")

Through the years, out of that house of worship, has come a multitude of ministers, Dad included and also my uncles James Holbrook and Willard Holbrook. In fact Quickstep, (which is located near Alger, Ohio) is the mother church of all Penetcostal Churches of God in the state of Ohio.

One would think that a church which has produced many outstanding ministers would be made up of perhaps hundreds of people. Not so with Quickstep. Through the years it has remained a charming, rural church with a colorful legacy. It's members, which number about one hundred people, are unpretentious, homespun, hard working folk whose ancestors migrated to Hardin County Ohio from Kentucky over a century ago.

We wanted Dad's funeral to be done with dignity as the final tribute to a saint gone to glory. In spite of that, I must admit that I cried. Cried? *Baloney!* I sobbed on Mary's shoulder, soaking it to the bone. I seemed to take Dad's passing harder than my siblings.

Why? That is because I had so many regrets and unfinished business with Dad. I suddenly realized (much to late) that my father, the man who had begotten me, was to me a little more than a stranger.

Prior to the funeral family members were permitted to place something in the coffin with Dad, a present of sorts. I gave Dad my possession, a turquoise ring which I had brought from Arizona in 1977. The ring had only been off my finger not more than five times.

As I placed the ring under Dad's cold, lifeless hand I suddenly became aware that I had never before given him a gift of any kind. That is when I lost it. I bent over sobbing as my gut wrenched in a deluge of emotion.

It is tough to face the death of a parent, especially if the one you lost is a person you have loved and respected. I held my father in high regard, but I had never told him so. I esteemed him for the way he stood by what God told him to do, regardless of the circumstances or ramifications. I respected his preaching the Gospel of Jesus Christ in a little a little storefront podunk church in one of the worst sectors in Cleveland.

In winter gangs of young boys would come past Dad's church and one would hold the door open as the others threw snowballs at him as he was preaching. Dad would tell those boys that God loved them and he did too.

My dad was an outstanding man of God and here I sit at my desk weeping because I am telling you what I should have years ago. Don't neglect your parents and grandparents. We tend to think they will be around forever and suddenly they are gone.

But as for Dad, *Semper Fideles.*

Your

Eternal Friend

Dear Judy:

Forgive this intrusion. But I couldn't rest until at long last I told you goodbye. I mean it was quite a shock. You were here in June and gone by September. The diabetes took you fast didn't it? Did it hurt? Please lie if you have to and say no. Please?

Didn't your Daddy pray? He was a preacher wasn't he? I thought sick people get better when preachers prayed. What went wrong? I asked your brother about that and he said that God works in mysterious ways. I think he is right. I mean if were understood everything about God he wouldn't be God anymore. If I had all the answers **I'd** be God. Anyway, knowing that you are with God makes me happy. I know that God is better to you than anybody.

Two years after you went away I met up with your brother at the Allen County Fair. We had some time to talk that day and all he seemed to speak of was his dream of becoming a professional landscaper. I couldn't understand how anyone could get so enthused about shrubbery and rolls of muddy sod. But, he had a goal and he went for it. That is something I never did. I thought goal setting was dooming yourself to a life of frustration. I discovered much too late that an aimless life *without* goals is a life of frustration.

I thought he was just blowing smoke from a pipe dream, but you know, now he owns a very successful lawn and garden center.

Anyway, my memories of you you are as cracked and faded as the fifth grade school picture you gave me when we were both young. When Mary gets over there you can tell her what a stinker I used to be. Have you seen Mrs. Jenkins, our fifth grade teacher? If you do see her say that I am well and doing fine.

Your eternal friend,
Adam

Dear Diane:

I recall with fondness that balmy summer night so long ago in the summer of '69. Oliver's song came over the radio as we rode in the back seat of Rhonda's red rag top Chevrolet on our way home from Lakota. Do you remember I held you close and we were young, much to young to know about love. Yet it seemed so right with my arm around your frail shoulders as we, half asleep, and Rhonda at the helm pressed on though the night. The show we sang and the thunderous applause were but fading embers compared to your warm breath on my shoulder.

I loved you then but didn't know enough about love to understand just why you drove my senses wild. You were but a little girl and I was not much more than a child. At that age love is pure and undefiled. You remained a little girl but I became a man in that summer of '69.

I never once held you again even though I wanted to. We lost the magic of that night and went our separate ways: you to follow your lofty dreams and I to chase the sky. For many years I thought of you from time to time but never heard your name. Then one evening Mary and I were talking to our friend Treda in a public place and she told us you had been killed in an automobile accident. Later, at home, I hid myself from my new bride and wept.

Late this night when I heard Oliver sing good morning to someone named Star Shine, I was reminded of that sweet summer night night so long ago – before either one of us had given away our innocence. When I occasionally hear that song, I am swept away by nostalgic recollections of that soft summer's night in Rhonda's convertible.

Thanks for the memory Diane.

Your eternal friend
Adam

Dear Marcie:

Just what were you thinking of so long ago when you sat grinning at me from atop those piles of dirt? Don't answer that question! I believe I know what was on your mind. Don't think if we had ever forged a meaningful relationship it should have had more auspicious beginnings? Maybe not. I thought you were cute, but you know that at times I did have some shy ways.

Still, though, I wish I had gotten to know you better. After your dad bought that farm over near Harrod I saw a good deal more of you. At least then I could admire you from a distance every day at school.

That one summer I worked very hard at helping my step-father install that septic tank at your house. I worked with one eye on the house just in case you were watching. You knew that, didn't you.

Remember how your brothers use to build those crude looking, rough wooden wannabe soap box derby cards? We had no hill so we pushed them on a dusty dirt track around your mother's garden. Remember? I was kind of short but I could still push as fast as Ralphie, a boy from up the road. I rarely got to drive because I was the only one who could keep up with the long legged Ralphie.

You really hurt me once. Do you remember the day I called and asked if you would go with me on a double date with Rhonda and her boyfriend? Yeah, I sure remember! You told me to go to Hell. I was devastated. At least I had worked up the nerve to ask you out and you gave me an answer like *that.* A simple no would have been more gracious don't you think?

I accompanied Rhonda and Glenn to the drive in movie anyway, but I didn't enjoy myself. I couldn't get interested in the movie because I was thinking of you and alone in the front seat munching stale popcorn while Rhonda and Glenn were in the back necking. Speaking of Glenn, have you seen him? Just thought I'd ask.

I was hurt, but it helped a lot when I saw you the following day. You wee definitely embarrassed when you found out it was me who called and not that other guy who also called himself Butch.

I still can still remember how red your face turned when you said, "I'll go out with you any time!" It's not that I held that misunderstanding against you, but I never again asked you for a date. I'm sorry I didn't but being told to go to Hell for whatever reason makes a guy a little gun shy.

After graduation we sort of lost track of one another. I was so broken up after splitting up with a girl I truly loved that I wouldn't have been much fun to be with anyway. I had made that idiotic decision to join the Air Force (inspired by temporary insanity no doubt.) But I know you'd have been a much better catch.

I was home on leave when you had that accident. I was so numb to my own feelings that I didn't shed any tears right away. That came later.

I can't help believing that if I had asked you out again, we would possibly have stayed together. If you had been my girl you would have been somewhere else the night that guy slammed his car into a concrete pillar.

Do you see much of him now? I know he's a nice guy. Any young man you would take an interest in has to be special. Anyway, I thought I'd write and at least explain why I never asked for another date.

Maybe we can get together when I get over there. Is it a date?

Your eternal friend
Butch

Dear Joe:

I was working on a piece about the Westminster of old, that is in the 1960's, when we were growing up there. It was coming hard because my thoughts kept turning to you. No writings about the Westminster of yesteryear with the mention of Height's pond. I was thinking of that pond and the good times we had there so I thought at long last I would write you a line.

I am going to tell you that our friendship remains an indelible part of my life. You have permanently impressed me in so many ways that I am at a loss to explain them all.

Allow me to start by saying that you seemed to have all of the answers. You quickly spanned the baffling problems that I had found to be confusing and irksome. You possessed wisdom far beyond your years and I could have learned much more from you if you hadn't gone away. Responsibility in one of those things. You were solid and steady. I faltered in body and mind.

You should remember that as a youngster I was a fraidy-cat type who could, at times be downright stupid. I couldn't drive a nail straight I was terrified to climb to climb the massive tree on the riverbank where you and our buddy Dave were involved in a perpetual tree house remodeling project. I was far too fearful of cutting myself to use a handsaw and when I did muster the moxie to try my cut in the board was invariably crooked. Many times I had rendered a once fine piece of lumber utterly worthless.

I know there were times in which Dave would like to have pulverized my face for being so disgustingly ignorant, but you never once lost your composure. You gave new meaning to the age old expression, "Good Joe."

I always had a knack for getting others in trouble and you were certainly not excluded from the list of boys who followed me in harebrained schemes and found much trouble. At least one of our Halloween pranks went much too far and became an act of vandalism instead of just a youthful prank.

I recall the early spring day you and I went back to the pond and boarded the raft your dad had built and kept at the pond. I know you remember. We were in the middle of the pond and I purposefully dropped the anchors into the water. Our combined strength proved inadequate to raise them so you swam to the shore in water temperatures near forty degrees. I attempted to do the same and nearly drowned. You threw me a life preserver, but still had to dive in and swim almost back to the raft to get me. Was I a dummy, or what?

How about the mini-vacation we took to southern Ohio with ours sister and your mom? I proved to be nothing but trouble the whole trip. When we got back to your house you caught me cheating at Rack-O and I punched you in the nose. You mom really had to restrain herself from wringing my neck. Looking back, I wouldn't have blamed her if she had.

Do you see what I have written so far? Foolishness! Pure, simple, unadulterated *foolishness!* Through all of that and more I never seemed to ruffle your feathers. You never seemed to be annoyed nor displayed the slightest speck of frustration. That, my dear friend is the mark of a man. I am pleased to report the years have given me a measure of that intangible, but vital commodity called wisdom.

Can you forgive me for being such an ignoramus? I am not making excuses for myself but try to remember that I, as an infant, suffered brain damage due to an illness. In fact I have been learning through time to use other brain cells to compensate for the ones which were destroyed years ago. But I loved you for the way you seemed to know that as a child I wasn't "right." You gave me plenty of space to learn, experience and grow from our association.

But let's, for a moment regress to the good times. Do you recall when you, Dave and our other comrade, Roger were just for the heck of it digging foxholes in those mounds of dirt left over from the construction of your house so long ago? Do you recall what you said to me when I asked you to share your hole in the ground? You handed me a shovel and sad, "Dig your own." That suggestion was succinct, but profound. From that I learned never to ask others to do what I am to lazy to do for myself.

Do you recall the two man all night monopoly games? How about the Crazy Eights tournaments at your cousin's house that sometimes lasted until five in the morning? Do you feel the overwhelming warmth from deep inside, as I do, when I think of all the New Year's Eves helping our sisters babysit your little cousins? One New Year's Eve I walked to your house and arrived just at midnight. You and Roger were firing shotguns out the patio door, celebrating the arrival of 1970.

In our high school years when I learned you were taking flying lessons, I knew then you would be a topnotch pilot. You were responsible and mature. After you had earned your pilot's license and I flew with you, I was genuinely impressed. Your every move was deliberate and skillful. I recall how you would take your girlfriend flying over our farm. I would wave and you would dip your wings as a way of saying "Hi."

I learned of the plans you has to join the Air Force and I was ecstatic. You would have made an outstanding Air Force pilot. The military needed all the men like you it could get. But the, you would have no doubt succeeded in anything you set your heart to do.

I was in the Air Force taking my medical training at Sheppard Air Force Base in Texas when I phoned my Mom and she told me about your crash. It had happened weeks before, but Mom couldn't decide when or how to tell me. Christmas was fast approaching and Mom knew she should tell me before I came home on holiday furlough.

Mom delivered the news to me that you, your dad, your grandfather and another man had been killed in an airplane crash in Missouri as you were en route to Texas on a hunting trip. She sad it was in a blinding snow storm and Joe had turned the aircraft around and was returning to the airport when they all were killed.

My blood went cold and the telephone booth seemed to be suddenly very hot. My knees were weak, but I unsteadily made may way back to my room in the barracks. My roommate, Sam said I looked pale. I told him what had happened and he understood why I was shaken.

We had big plans for the Air Force didn't we Joe. You were going to be a pilot and I was going to be a nurse. Neither of us made it, did we?

You know, as you were often flying over our farm so many years ago, I often thought of painting the words, HI JOE on the roof of our woodshed. Sometimes I get the idea that I would still like to do that.

Your eternal friend,
Butch

Dear Ernie:

What were you trying to prove? You knew that beer always made you sleepy and after ten hours of hard work you went out drinking. Why did you do that?

At our Labor Day picnic you puzzled me just a little by the things you had to say. But I was happy for you and looking forward to your wedding day. Laura was different from the other girls you brought around and she had such darling little daughter too. I could see that you truly loved them both. I knew you had at last found that pot of gold you had been seeking for most of your life.

Did it astonish you to discover that true gold is not to be found in Fort Knox? What took you so long? I had that figured out before we left grade school.

Do you remember New Year's Eve of '71? That brunette and her sister got us sooo drunk. Your dad was really steamed when you couldn't find your car. How about that rainy midnight ride through Farout Park in my '64 Opal? I don't suppose you could forget the day I broke that other kid's nose. Yeah, and your mom cried as she peeled that bloody tee shirt off my back.

I always loved your mom. She never had much to say, but I can still hear her shouting up the stairs, "ERNIE!..... RAY!......RICKY!(a pause of seven seconds) BUTCH!"

Does she still wake you that way?

How could we ever forget those little gems my mom taught us. Things like "You can pick your friends and you can pick your nose, but you can't pick your friend's nose." Everybody sure got a charge out of that at Shirley's birthday party.

I could have crowned you (and it wouldn't have been King Edward) that Sunday morning you threw my alarm clock across the room. How else could I have I gotten you up? You were obligated to help your little brother Rick deliver newspapers.

Speaking of Rick, do you recall how he loved to play that Paul McCartney "Ram" album at full throttle at seven every morning you and I had been drinking the night before?

*"HAAAAAANDS ACROSS THE WATER!!
HAAAAAANDS ACROSS THE SKY!"*

Nothing against Paul McCartney mind you, but I learned to dislike that sng. Nowadays when I hear it I smile.

How about all of our bawdy song? We were a pair of song writers weren't we? Gems like "roll Your Leg Over" and "Meet me at the Ice Cream Stand Next to the Wesleyan Church" rolled from my pen and your guitar. Paul Williams! Eat your heart out!

Can I fight song just one more time? It always made us laugh and I am truly in need of a good belly laugh.

We never stagger!
We never fall!
We sober up on pure alcohol!

Send our highballs to the sky
And guzzle to vic-to-ry!

Hmmmm.....that song loses something when you sing while you are sober.

But Ernie, you had a magnetic personality. Everyone said so. There was so much good in you. You know as well as I that our friendship was not based solely upon chasing the ladies and our collection of ribald drinking songs. We had many late night talks around a camp fire. Those were our blood-brotherly times.

Your foremost goal in life was to become wealthy, which I thought was a waste of time and energy but I loved your benevolent attitude. You fed my family when I had no grocery money. You drove long distances at your own expense driving me to and from psychiatric hospitals.

I could go on, but you know, sometimes you really torqued me off. I mean, you tried to hustle every girl I had and sometimes succeeded. That's all right, you lecherous fool!

I could get bitter about my lost girlfriends and curse the day we befriended one another. but throwing away a thirty three year friendship over a few floozies is not worth it. I'm sure you know by now that life is much too short for that sort of imbecility

Yes, in spite of your faults, I loved you as a brother. That's why it hurt so badly when Laura called at four-thirty that morning and told us you were gone. What really sent me down the tubes is when the next day I switched on the television news and found there had been a fire after the crash.

I just can't understand how you could have had us at nearly 150 miles an hour on Labor Day and then a few days later lost it on a long curve at half that speed. But beer in any quantity always made you sleepy. Is that what happened?

I know I'll be awake for a good long while, but I am going to bed anyway. God bless you and good night my bro. Give my warmest regards to your mom.

Your eternal friend,
Butch

Post Script

April 15, 2003

I thought this book was completed, that every jot and tittle was in place, that uis until a few weeks ago. That short amount of seems for like several decades. You see, early on the morning of February 12, 2003 Robert J. Aab died. Until now I have found it a very difficult to write about Bob's death.

As many of you know, some of us have a hard time dealing with death. The words are coming hard. Please bear with me.

As you may know, Bob raised me from the time I was two years of age. In those forty six years we had our share of disagreements, some of them bitter, but the love we had for one another never died. That is one of the characteristics of love, it can be tried by fire many times but never is it devoured by the flames.

As I stood beside Bob's flag draped coffin stroking his cold lifeless hands, I pondered the deeds those hands had done on their eighty one years of life. They were hands that had worked hard for long hours in order to provide a living for out family. They were hands which we used to tan my hide, when I had, as a child, misbehaved. They were hands that could be both sterne and loving. Those hands could swing a belt with the best of them one minute and cradle a sick kitten the next. I had seen those hands drive spikes all day and then gently feed a baby that evening.

Those hands were employed to fight and defeat Adolph Hitler during the dark dasys of WWII. In that struggle for human freedom Bob had won as Bronze Star, Purple Heart and the Oak Leaf Cluster. He was seriously wounded twice.

Yes, Bob's hands were those of a *real* man, a true hero who had done his duty to God, his family and his country. He had done so with strength, courage and dignity.

Those hands were now chilled and motionless as I held them. Yes, Bob was a genuine hero who had, no doubt been welcomed into heaven by a multitude of grateful souls.

Printed in the United States
By Bookmasters